AF413216

A General's Letters to His Son on Minor Tactics

Anonymous

Writat

This edition published in 2020

ISBN : 9789390439072 (Hardback)
I

Design and Setting By
Writat
(An Imprint of Vij Publishiing Group)
www.vijbooks.com
contact@vijpublishing.com

Table of Contents

PREFACE

It has very forcibly been brought home to me that not only young officers joining their units from training establishments, but also those who have been in France and have come back wounded, are often very ignorant on those points in minor tactics which they have not learnt through actual experience on the battlefield, and that this is especially the case with regard to the proper control of fire. The battlefield is an expensive place to acquire knowledge which can be gained elsewhere, and it behooves us to do all we possibly can to train our young commanders under peace conditions for the ordeals they will have to encounter in the presence of the enemy.

Training which in ordinary times would form the course of study for years now has to be crammed into a few months, and it stands to reason that much which is essential remains unlearnt.

I have generally found that the best way to train young officers in minor tactics is by giving them as realistically as possible little problems to solve, and afterwards in the presence of their comrades to discuss their proposed dispositions and then to tell them clearly what they ought to have done, giving reasons for every step taken.

Where it is possible actually to carry out the exercise with troops, this is still better, so long as it is all done quickly, as this impresses the lesson to be learnt more strongly on the minds of the students.

Many men who are in other ways excellent instructors have not the facility for constructing problems with *a point*, and this being the case, it has occurred to me that I may be generally helping the training of young officers by publishing these letters which are written in continuation of those I addressed to my son on obtaining his commission. The importance of the subject with which they deal is self-evident. Unless the arrow-head, the platoon, be sharp, that is, unless the leader be skilful as well as brave, the little combat will not be won, and it is the sum of the little combats which spells the result of the battle.

There is not a word in this little book which transgresses the spirit of the training manuals and official instructions now in force.

"X. Y. Z."

LETTER I

December 1, 1917.

My dear Dick,—

It is now nearly nine months since I wrote the last of my letters of advice to you, and since then you have yourself been in France and have had many experiences and hairbreadth escapes.

I am very thankful that your wound is only a slight one, and am glad that within a couple of months you will probably once more be able to take your place in the fighting-line, for that is where your country demands your presence. It behoves you, in the meantime, to seize every opportunity of studying your profession and familiarising yourself as far as possible with the different positions in which you may be placed, so that when you meet a similar situation in the field you may recognise it for what it really is, in spite of the surroundings in which it is dressed, and may thus be more likely to solve it properly than would be the case if you were dealing with a problem which you had never thought over before. It would be difficult to exaggerate the importance of the results which may depend on your correctly answering the questions put to you on the field of battle. These questions become more complex and more varied as the responsibility of an officer's position increases, but in the case of a junior officer they are seldom very difficult, and all that is required to deal with them properly is a little common sense and a cool head combined with courage and determination.

It is on the result of the many little fights of which an action is composed that the result of a battle depends. The brilliant strategy of a commander-in-chief and the fine tactics of a divisional commander cannot bear fruit unless the troop-leading of the companies is well carried out, and in the same way good troop-leading will prevent a defeat being turned into a rout. Individual gallantry, valuable as it may be, is bound to be thrown away if unaccompanied by skill. The experiences you have undergone should render you more capable of assimilating the requisite knowledge than you were nine months ago.

Before I proceed further, I will mention a few axioms which can seldom be neglected without bad results accruing. Some of these seem so self-evident that it would appear to be unnecessary to state them, nevertheless they are all of them continually transgressed.

1. Impress on your men the importance of adjusting their sights correctly. On a peace field-day this axiom is sometimes neglected, and in the excitement of action it is often entirely forgotten.

2. Keep your men together unless there is some very definite object for not doing so, and only detach them for protective services, *i.e.* advance guards, etc.

3. Infantry mounted officers are apt to forget that their horses are given to them in order to give them more mobility. There are many occasions on which, by cantering on and making arrangements previous to the arrival of the unit which they command, they can save a great deal of valuable time and often much marching and counter-marching.

4. Never allow the pace in front to be hurried on a march. It is much easier to march at the head than at the rear of a column.

5. Before opening fire, carefully consider the situation. If you feel certain of being able to deal with the enemy, let him approach close before disclosing yourself, and then destroy him. If, on the contrary, he is

so much superior to you that you cannot hope to be able to do this, you should open at a long range, but in these circumstances do not hurry the rate of fire to begin with. It takes an exceptional man to fire more than 200 rounds in a short space of time without being shaken.

6. It is a sound rule always to pursue the line of action which your opponent does not wish you to pursue. If, for instance, in the circumstances mentioned in the above paragraph the enemy open fire on you at a long range, you may presume that he does so in order to keep you at arm's length, and if you halt you are probably doing what he wishes you to do.

7. However small your party may be when acting independently, it is responsible for its own protection, and it should always have an advance guard or its equivalent.

8. Whenever you have an opportunity of doing so, and the tactical situation allows of it, check your ranges by firing at an auxiliary mark where you can see the splash of your bullet, such as a dusty road or water.

9. When you have ascertained the correct distances of the object, make a range-card and pass on your information to neighbouring troops.

10. If you see a good opportunity of inflicting loss on the enemy, but it is impracticable to check the range, use combined sights.

11. Remember that if the target you are shooting at is large enough and you know the range, you can inflict heavy losses with rifle and machine-gun fire at ranges well over 2,000 yards.

12. Do not forget to make use of the map when estimating a range.

13. Although the secret of success in an engagement is the proper co-operation of the different

arms of the service, the platoon commander must not cry out for artillery assistance when he has the means of carrying out his task in his own platoon, which, with its riflemen, its Lewis gunners, its bombers, and its rifle bombers, is, in itself, a miniature division. In an action where telephonic communication has broken down this rule applies with special force.

14. Above all things, impress on your men the enormous power of their rifle. I have heard many stories of men not firing at all because they hoped the enemy would come within *bombing range*. I have also heard of bodies of German troops streaming across the open unfired at because no order was given. I have also heard of machine guns stopping a German advance, whilst infantry who were lying down beside them did not fire a shot.

15. Rifle grenades and bombs both have their proper uses, and in trench fighting it would be difficult to get on without them. The former are also excellent for giving covering fire whilst a post is being rushed; but if the infantryman's worth be 100, of this 100, 85 per cent. belongs to his rifle and bayonet, 10 per cent. to his rifle grenade, and 5 per cent. at the outside to his bomb.

16. Never miss an opportunity to reorganise your company or platoon, as the case may be, ready for the next emergency.

17. After capturing a trench or work, get your Lewis guns into position without any delay. From a small front they can bring a great fire to bear, and they must be given the best position. Under the protection given by them, the remainder of your command must consolidate.

(For consolidation, see note to Scheme 7.)

18. Your duty towards the enemy is your duty towards your neighbour reversed. Think how he could make himself most objectionable to you and act in this manner towards him.

19. Always be certain that you understand your orders, and if you are in doubt never hesitate to ask and make certain, even should your commanding officer have a short temper.

20. If you are detached for any specific purpose you should always rejoin your unit when you have accomplished what you were told to do.

21. Do not fail to give negative information. Young officers are very apt to neglect this. It may be of great importance to a commanding officer to know that a certain place is not held by the enemy, and this is just the kind of information that his patrol leaders are apt to forget to send him.

22. Always insist on any verbal order you may give being repeated to you by the recipient before he leaves your presence.

23. In a retirement you send men to the rear with orders to take up another position to protect your retirement; always see that they are accompanied by a competent leader, or when the last party falls back they will very likely find that their retirement is unsupported.

Try to remember these axioms. My subsequent letters will be founded on their application.

Your affectionate father,
"X. Y. Z."

LETTER II

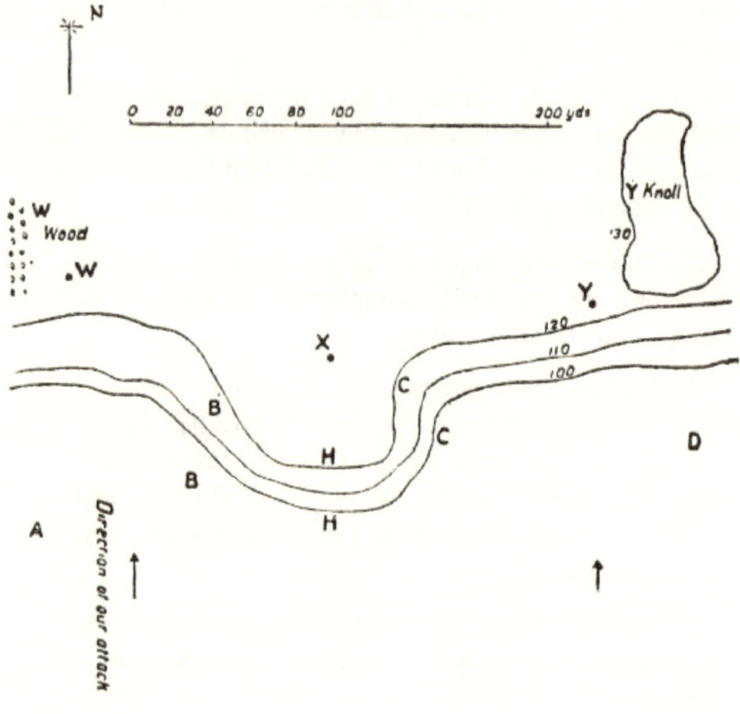

W X Y are Pill Boxes

W & Y have been captured by us   X still holds out

W X Y are Pill Boxes

W & Y have been captured by us **X** still holds out

December 7, 1917.

MY DEAR DICK,—

I will now proceed to set you a few problems in illustration of the axioms which I gave you at the end of my last letter.

The first will be on the subject of taking a German pill-box, for I have heard of many instances of a pill-box holding up the advance of a whole brigade for a very considerable period. I have also heard how many gallant but badly devised attempts to carry it have failed, and the lives of officers and men have been sacrificed in vain, and how eventually a better commanded platoon has succeeded in taking it with very little loss.

PROBLEM 1

W, *X*, and *Y* are three pill-boxes about 150 yards apart. We are attacking in the direction [20] of the arrows, that is, in a northerly direction.

Our men following close behind the barrage took pill-boxes *W* and *Y*; but, partly owing to the conformation of the ground and partly for other reasons, we failed to take *X*, and this pill-box is now holding up the whole of our advance between *W*, wood, and *Y*, knoll, with a machine gun, which is being fired from the inside of the pill-box, and which sweeps the whole ground between these points so effectively that directly we attempt to advance our men are mown down.

It is apparent that *X* has only one machine gun in action, though this is a very efficient one.

From the contours on the sketch, it is evident that the ground is convex in formation, that is, that it is nearly flat between X and H^1, but that it slopes rapidly between H^1 and H, between B^1 and B, and between C^1 and C.

The slopes are covered with brushwood. The ground between contour 120 and the pill-box is meadow land.

The platoon originally told off to attack *X* was wiped out.

Problem.

You have been ordered to take X with your platoon and to do so as quickly as possible. When you receive these orders you are yourself at H, and, as you will see from the sketch, are not under fire from X.

What steps will you take to carry out your orders?

Do not enter into an elaborate dissertation, but give short, concise orders, and if you desire to do so, append a short statement saying why you gave these orders.

Action considered Correct.

As there is only one machine gun in action, if X be attacked simultaneously from B^1 and C^1, either one party or the other should succeed in getting to the rear of the pill-box and blowing in the door.

Orders.

No. 4 Section with the Lewis gun will choose a position somewhere to the north of H, and on my signal will open a rapid fire on the loopholes of the pill-box at X. No. 3 Section will choose a position near B^1, and when the Lewis gun opens fire, they will open a rapid rifle-grenade fire on X. One minute after the Lewis gun has opened, No. 1 Section will rush in from C^1 and No. 2 Section from B^1.

* * * * *

I am aware that in the foregoing problem I have made the task of the platoon commander a very simple one. I wished, however, to avoid any points of controversy. If the ground should not be so advantageous for your attack as that above depicted, the principle, viz. movement combined with fire, still remains the same. You should bring a converging attack to bear and advance your men under cover of the fire of your rifle grenades and Lewis guns, and by pushing men forward from one shell-crater to another, you should generally be able to achieve your object if your plan be evolved on sound principles. It is also possible that smoke bombs could be used with advantage if the wind be favourable.

The above problem is one which has often been put to young officers on the battlefield, and they have not by any means always given a satisfactory answer to it, simple as it is.

Your affectionate father,
"X. Y. Z."

LETTER III

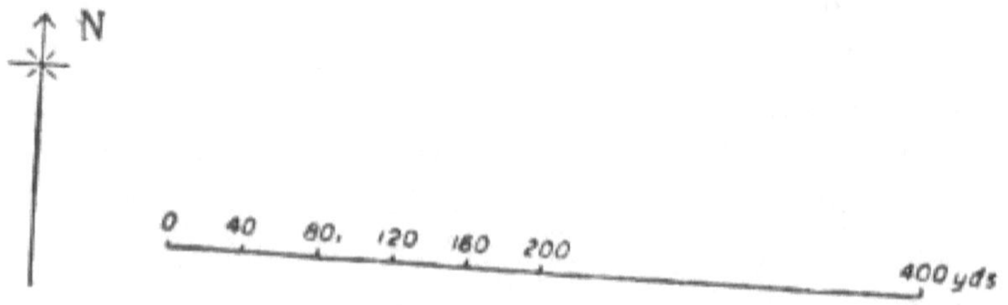

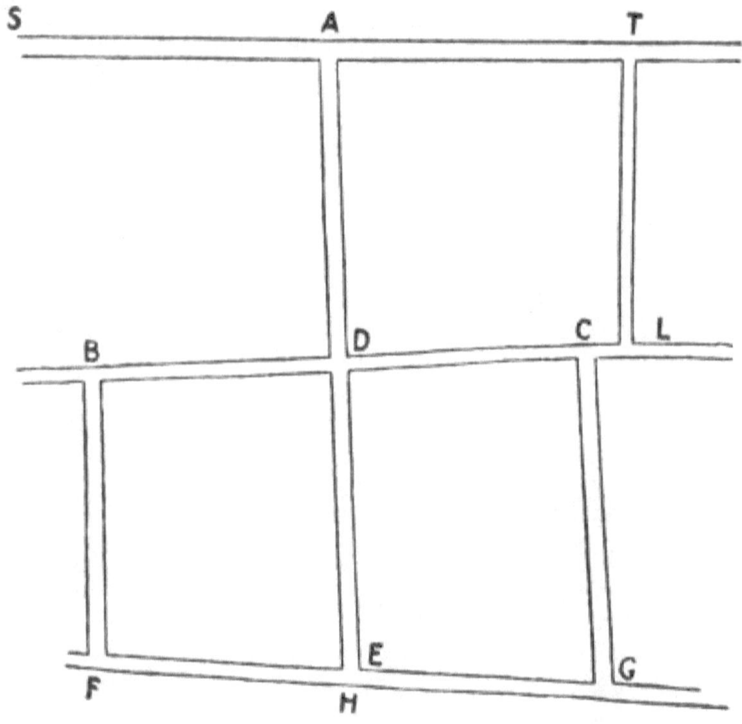

December 15, 1917.

My dear Dick,—

Since the early days of the campaign there has been but little fighting in towns or villages which have not previously been so knocked about that they could better be designated ruins than habitable places, but in the event of an advance on a large scale towns and villages are certain to be the scenes of severe combats. I will therefore give you three little problems in street-fighting. When you have read them, the points I call attention to will probably seem to you so self-evident that you will wonder that I have considered it worth while to comment on them. Nevertheless, I am not quite sure that you will give what I consider to be the correct answers to all of them, if you do not turn over the page and look at the solutions I have given, before stating your own.

PROBLEM 2

The brigade to which you belong has entered a town from a southerly direction, and you are opposed by an enemy who has entered it from a northerly direction.

The company of which you are in command has been allotted the ground between the roads *B F*, *C G*, both inclusive, your flanks are protected, the streets are about thirty feet broad with pavements five feet broad, houses run all along the streets.

Answer the following Questions.

(*a*) If you were to tell off a section to prevent the enemy advancing along the street *B F* from a northerly direction, which side of the street would it be best for them to occupy, and why?

(*b*) Your men occupy the streets *B D* and *D C*, but no man can show his face in the street *A H*, which is covered by machine guns and snipers firing from near *A*, and all men attempting to cross the road at *D* have been shot. Several houses in the street *B D* have been knocked down by shell fire.

In this street there are six empty wagons and in the houses in the street there is to be found furniture of all descriptions, as well as ropes, harness, and stables, with some horses in them. You are anxious to place a barricade across the street *A H* at *D*, so as to enable you to use the crossing at *D*. How should you set about making this barricade?

(*c*) There is a house at *H* looking right down the street *A H*. Whereabouts in this house should you put your Lewis gun, and why?

Solutions.

(*a*) On the western side, because your men, shooting out of the windows in a northerly direction, would then fire from their right shoulders without exposing their bodies.

(*b*) Fill the wagons with rubble from the houses which have been knocked down. Fasten sacking or sheets on to the wagon, so as to give cover from view between the body of the wagon and the ground. Throw a string attached to a brick across the street. By means of this, pull over a rope and attach the wagons to this rope, and thus pull them into the position you require.

(*c*) At the back of a room in the house, where you can see but cannot be seen, firing through the window. If you choose a window near the top of the house and put the Lewis gun on a table some distance back in the room, you will probably be able to fire over the barricade which you are thinking of constructing at *D*.

I have put you three definite and very simple questions with regard to street-fighting, for it may often happen that correct action on the spur of the moment when a village is first entered may result in ground being easily gained which would otherwise entail heavy fighting and serious loss to capture.

Street-fighting is a very big subject, and as a rule it gradually develops into underground warfare.

Villages entered during a battle often have snipers in the top stories or on the roofs of the houses, and these are places in which you may also place a few good shots with great advantage. This is an illustration of the advisability of doing to the enemy what you do not like his doing to you.

I will send you another problem next week.

Your affectionate father,
"X. Y. Z."

LETTER IV

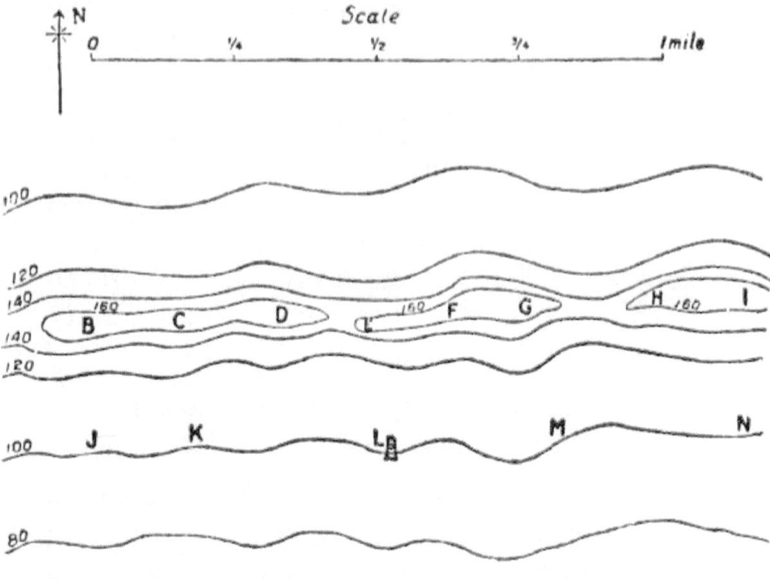

December 22, 1917.

My dear Dick,—

You have told me that you have once or twice temporarily commanded a company and have asked me whether I think there is any advantage in a young and active company commander being mounted.

In another part of your letter you ask whether I think a defensive position should be taken up on a forward or on a reverse slope.

This latter is a very big question and one on which many pages could be written, but I shall confine myself here to saying that it is imperative to hold the crest line in order to get observation, but that, owing to the crest line and forward slope being so much more vulnerable by artillery fire than is the reverse slope, there are many advantages in constructing the main line of defence well behind the crest.

I find now that I have tried in a few words [32] to answer your second question before dealing with the first one. The object of giving you a horse is, firstly, to enable you to move about more rapidly, and consequently to do your duty better; and secondly, because a company commander's work really begins when the march is over. It is infinitely more important that he should be fresh than that any other man in the company should be so. Again, by riding on in front and making proper arrangements for bivouacs or billets, he may save weary men much marching and counter-marching, and, what is even more important, he will on other occasions, by being able to push on in front, save half an hour by thinking out proper tactical dispositions before his men arrive. I will now give you a little problem which will, I think, illustrate the two questions which you have asked me. You must, nevertheless, remember that there can be no hard-and-fast rule as to where a position should be taken up. We cannot alter the ground to suit our formation, and therefore our formations must be made to suit the ground. The proper way to hold ground when the object is [33] to fight a rearguard action is quite different from the way it should be held to fight a battle *à l'outrance*, and all I will commit myself to doing is to give my advice as to how a certain piece of ground should be held in certain given circumstances. I hope that the following problem will, to a certain extent, answer both your questions.

PROBLEM 3

An advance guard, of which the company you command forms part, has been pushed forward to seize a position of which the ridge *B-I* forms a part. The main body should reach the position some eight hours after your arrival there. You have been told that your first object is to prevent the enemy's cavalry seizing the position. The enemy's cavalry, accompanied by horse artillery, may be expected in the proximity of the position within an hour or so after your arrival, but it is unlikely that his infantry and field artillery will arrive much before your own main body. The time of the year is July, the hour is 4 p.m. The soil is sandy, but covered with[34] grass. You are riding at the head of your company, and are about two miles from the crest when a staff officer accompanied by the adjutant rides up to you and you receive the following instructions:

"Our cavalry have reached the crest of the ridge *B C D E F G H I* without encountering opposition. You will be responsible for the front from *E* to *I*, both inclusive, until the main body arrives, and must make immediate arrangements for securing it against attack by hostile cavalry and horse artillery. Not a minute is to be lost. You will also do your best to prepare the front allotted to you for defence against a strong infantry attack which the enemy will probably deliver, though it is unlikely that he will be in a position to do so before dawn to-morrow."

Question 1.

What would you do on receipt of these orders?

Action considered Correct.

You should save time by handing over command of your company and yourself cantering[35] on so as to examine the ground and carefully consider your plans before your company arrives. The line of argument you should adopt on arrival on the ridge should be: "My first object is to prevent cavalry, assisted by horse artillery, reaching the ridge, and not a single moment is to be lost in doing this.

"My second object is to consider carefully how the ground can best be prepared to resist a determined infantry attack early to-morrow morning. It is possible that the ridge may be subjected to shell fire soon after the arrival of my company, and I must make hay whilst the sun shines."

The conclusions you would come to as a result of this reasoning would probably be: "It is improbable that I shall be able to entrench the whole of my company before the enemy opens fire, but at all events I will try to make emplacements for my four Lewis guns on the ridge between E and I. They will thus be about eighty yards apart.

"I will use intensive labour to get these emplacements completed quickly."

By intensive labour is meant telling off three men to each tool used and ordering the man to dig with all his might and main for a couple of minutes or until he is tired, and then to hand his tool over to another man who is ready to receive it. By this means more work can be done in half an hour than is usually done in an hour. For periods of under an hour, when men are working against time to achieve some important object, intensive labour is an excellent method to adopt, but it is not suited for long tasks where its use would wear men out. It is especially applicable where the task worked at is so small that only a very limited number of men can work simultaneously.

"I will, at the same time, construct trenches connecting these Lewis gun posts. It is possible that the arrival of the enemy's guns will oblige me to relinquish work until the night, but the fact that the trenches have been commenced in the daytime will very much assist the men in their night work. I will afterwards construct supporting points at the farm *L* and between *M* and *N* on the reverse slope."

Question 2.

If you concur with these conclusions, what principle will govern your action in putting the farm into a state of defence? You will notice that the farm shows a bigger front to the east and the west than it does to the north and the south. It is constructed of strong masonry and has two stories.

Action which is considered Correct.

You should use the southern rooms in the farm for your machine guns rather than the northern ones, as you will there be more protected from shell fire. You must keep your defence as much below ground as possible, using cellars if they are available, and otherwise digging trenches inside the walls so as to have your loopholes a few inches above the ground level.

Construct head cover with strong baulks close over your heads, so that in the event of the whole building being brought down, it will not affect you, but only give you more cover from high-angle fire. If possible put wire round the northern end of the building. Arrange to flank the work between *M N*, which should in turn protect your front.

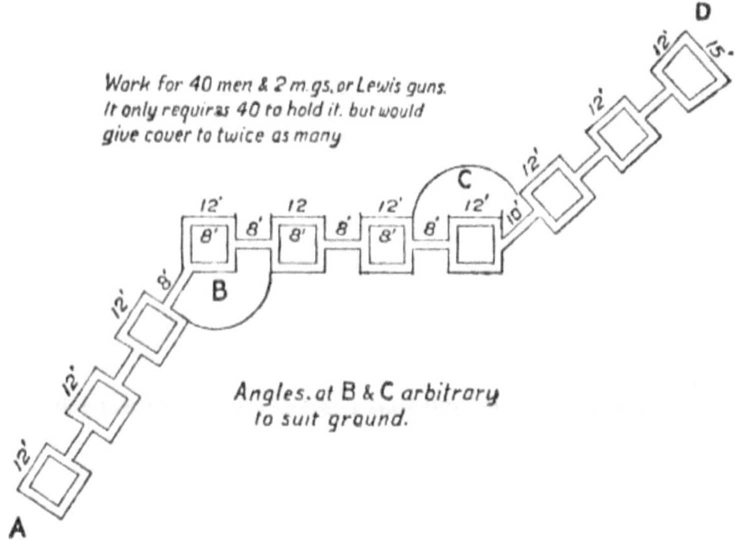

Work for 40 men & 2 m. gs. or Lewis guns. It only requires 40 to hold it, but would give cover to twice as many

Angles at B & C arbitrary to suit ground.

Question 3.

What description of work will you make between *M* and *N*?

Action considered Correct.

The best form of work to construct will be one made on the principle of that shown in the annexed diagram. As will be seen, this consists of a series of island traverses strung together more or less in the shape of an "S." The advantage of this is not only that it is suitable for all-round defence, but that the whole of the garrison can fire simultaneously in almost any direction, the weakest points being *A* and *D*. The work shown in the diagram would require a garrison of about forty men, but it could give cover to eighty. It is less vulnerable by artillery fire than almost any other form of work. It is an easy work to construct in so far that a large number of men can work at it at the same time without interfering with each other. The acuteness or obtuseness of the angles at *B* and *C* must depend entirely upon the ground, but it stands to reason that the more the angles approach right angles, the more is the work suitable for all-round defence.

The "crucifix" strong point is also a good pattern, but I think that the one that I have given you is better, as it is in every way a less satisfactory mark for the enemy artillery, and also gives you quite as good, if not better, opportunity of using all your rifles in every direction.

My next letter will contain a problem for a rearguard commander.

Your affectionate father,
"X. Y. Z."

LETTER V

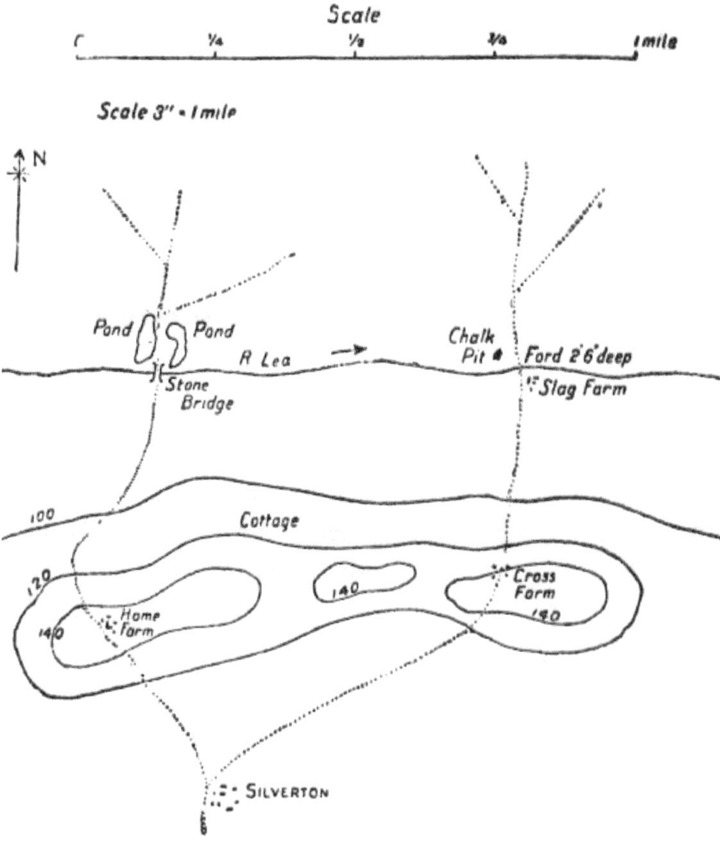

January 1, 1918.

My dear Dick,—

The last scheme I gave you dealt with the taking up of a position when an attack by a weak force was probable within an hour or so of your occupying it, and also with the strengthening of the same position for an expected attack by a stronger force twelve hours later. This one deals with a rearguard action. It is straightforward and plain. The object that troops fighting a rearguard action should have in mind is to keep the enemy at arm's length, to punish him severely if he is too bold, and at the same time not to compromise their own retreat, unless duty requires them to sacrifice themselves in order to save the main body. I will now set you the problem before I make my own solution too evident by my remarks. It is my intention to add a few more words at the end of this letter, but I do not wish you to look at them until you have written your own solution.

PROBLEM 4

The banks of the River Lea are steep, the river is about four feet six inches deep, except near the ford. The bottom is muddy. At the ford it is forty yards broad, in most other places about twenty yards. The fields on either side are firm. The roads shown on the sketch are dry and dusty. The soil is chalky. The depth of the river at the ford is two feet six inches. The date is June 20.

One of the orderlies attached to you reports that at Slag Farm there is a large quantity of wire, some of it barbed.

The brigade to which you belong is retiring in a southerly direction. The baggage moved in front of the brigade. The time is 5.30 p.m. You with your company, to which six mounted orderlies have been attached, are near Home Farm, the remainder of your battalion, which is in rear of the brigade, is passing through Silverton, when the adjutant rides up to you and gives you the following order:

"Information has been received that a hostile cavalry brigade is pursuing. You will take such steps as you may consider necessary to prevent the enemy crossing the River Lea between Stone Bridge and Slag Farm, both inclusive, until 7 p.m., at which hour you will be relieved by cavalry. You will be careful not to compromise your own retreat. Having accomplished your task, you will rejoin your unit."

Problem.

How do you appreciate the situation, and what steps will you take to carry out your instructions?

Solution considered Correct.

The River Lea is in all places within 800 yards of the ridge, and as the conditions are particularly favourable for fire action from the ridge, there is no necessity for you to place your men down the forward slope. The circumstances which render the situation so favourable for fire action are that it is practically impossible for the enemy's cavalry to cross the River Lea, except at the bridge or at the ford. The bridge and the road, with ponds on either side of it, just to the north of the bridge, form a defile 150 yards long, through which the enemy must pass. The ponds and the river also afford you an excellent opportunity to check the range by the splash of your bullets.

By filling the ford with wire you should also succeed in making that very difficult to cross. The great objection to putting men on the forward slope is that they will come under severe fire from the horse artillery which will accompany the cavalry, and that under cover of this fire the cavalry are much more likely to be able to cross than they would be if fired at from a concealed position on the ridge. Besides which all movement by men on the forward slope would be seen and the men themselves would not be able to retire until dark.

Orders.

1. Nos. 3 and 4 Platoons will proceed under Lieutenant Smith to the neighbourhood of Cross Farm, where they will take up the best positions they can find with the object of protecting the crossing of the River Lea.

It has been reported that a large quantity of wire, some of it barbed, is to be found at Slag Farm. Lieutenant Smith will take steps to obstruct the ford with this with the object of denying its use to the enemy.

2. No. 1 Platoon will take up a position near Home Farm and No. 2 Platoon near Hope Farm, also with the object of preventing the crossing of the River Lea.

3. No. 2 Platoon from Hope Farm will fire ranging shots on to the ford at Slag Farm, Chalk Pit, and the two road junctions to the north of the ford, and when the officer commanding the platoon is certain by the observation of his fire that he has obtained the correct ranges, he will pass this information to the officer commanding No. 1 Platoon.

The officer commanding No. 1 Platoon will range on the ponds near the bridge and on the road junction to the north of them, and will similarly pass the range chart to the officer commanding No. 2 Platoon. This ranging will be carried out at once in order that the ranging by Nos. 1 and 2 Platoons may be finished before the ranging is commenced by the officers commanding Nos. 3 and 4 Platoons, which will be carried out under the orders of Lieutenant Smith.

N.B.—I am quite aware that a company is supposed to carry a Barr & Stroud range-finder. Although this is an excellent instrument when it is in thorough order, there is really no such reliable range-finder as a rifle fired at a mark which will show the impact of the bullet.

* * * * *

In the proper solution of the foregoing scheme, everything really depends upon your fire orders. I am presuming that your men are fairly well trained with the rifle. I wish, of course, that all our men were trained up to the standard of the Old Contemptibles, but "Rome was not built in a day," nor can discipline and good marksmanship become part of a man's second nature as a result of only a few months' training. If, however, your men are reasonably good shots and can fire at least fifteen rounds a minute (they ought to fire twenty under peace conditions), in such cases as the above much more will depend upon whether you give correct fire orders than upon whether the men are first-class marksmen or only moderately good shots. You can compare a company of first-class marksmen to a Choke-bore gun which shoots farther and harder but requires a skilled game shot to use with advantage, whereas a company of moderately-trained shots would resemble an ordinary scatter gun, with which the ordinary shot would probably do more execution. If you give a range as 1,200 yards when it is only 1,000 yards and you have marksmen, no shots will fall on the object; whereas if your company were composed of third-class shots, the chances are that it would be well sprinkled with bullets. Do not think from this that I prefer the third-class shots, for that is very decidedly not the case; but if you have a highly finished weapon, you want a good man behind it, although in the hands of such a one it will do brilliant execution. If you have a company of good shots and are not certain of a range, your best plan is to fire with combined sights and thus to increase the depth of the fire-swept ground. This method, although in many cases the best to adopt, is bound to diminish the efficacy of your fire, for if the correct range be 1,200 yards and you fire one platoon at 1,000 yards, one at 1,100, one at 1,200, and one at 1,300, it stands to reason that you can only hope to get a quarter as many hits as you would do if you gave the whole four platoons the correct range; but even that is better than giving the range at 1,000 and missing the mark altogether. It is a bad plan to go "Nap" before you have looked at your hand. I shall later on give you certain little problems for solution in which I am of opinion that combined sights should be used. In the problem under consideration, however, their use would be absolutely wrong. You can check all the ranges by seeing the splash of the bullets either in the ponds, in the river, or on the Chalk Pit, and you should be content with nothing except the correct range. Young officers are always apt to consider that so long as they have taught their company to shoot fairly well, they have done their duty with regard to musketry. This is, in reality, by no means the case. The company is simply the sportsman's gun; the commander has to learn how to use it.

There are many circumstances under which a man has to pick out his own target, as, for instance, when the enemy is attacking, and here everything depends upon his individual marksmanship. There are, however, many other occasions in which if 10 per cent. of the effect depends upon whether the men are first-class marksmen or only ordinary decent shots, 90 per cent. will depend upon whether the officer gives fire orders properly adapted to the situation. The above problem is an illustration of this principle.

You should notice that in my solution I carefully arranged that the party comprised of Nos. 2 and 3 Platoons should not commence ranging until Nos. 1 and 2 Platoons had finished. Were they to fire simultaneously, confusion in the splashes made by the bullets would be the result.

Don't forget to hand over your range card to your relief.

Your affectionate father,
"X. Y. Z."

LETTER VI

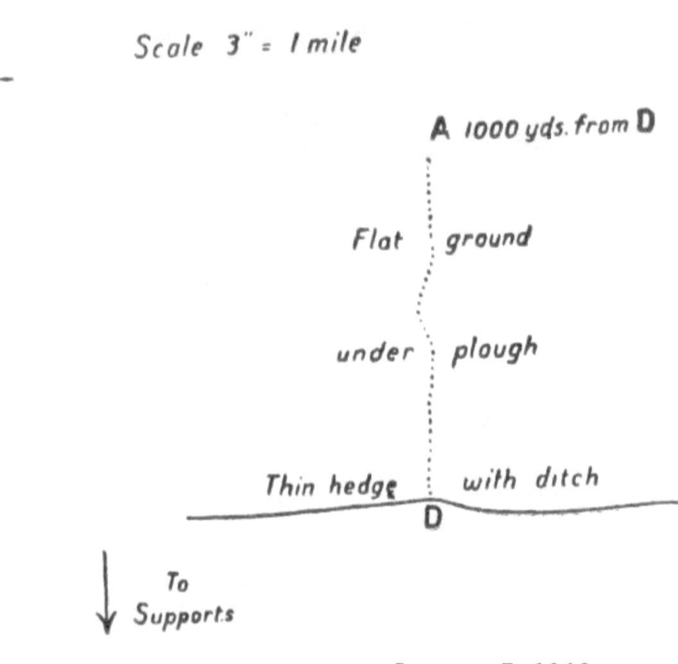

January 7, 1918.

PROBLEM 5*a*

My dear Dick,—

I will set you another problem.

The force to which you belong has made a night march. Your platoon now forms part of a new outpost line. You halted in a ditch at line marked *D*, with a thin hedge on the enemy's side of it, which gives you good cover from view. Your idea was to use this place as the headquarters of your picket, and as soon as it was thoroughly light to throw groups out in front. Your platoon consists of forty men and a Lewis gun. Soon after dawn and when your men are still in the trench at

D, you see what you take to be a strong platoon of the enemy advancing straight towards you from the north; a couple of groups of men are fifty yards in front, and the remainder of the platoon is advancing in fours along a country road, which passes close to your position. You see the platoon when it is at *A* about 1,000 yards off.

What action will you take?

Action considered Correct.

There seems to be every chance of your being able to ambuscade this party, and you should let it advance until the groups which the main body has in front of it are within fifty yards of your picquet. You should tell off a few men on the flanks to deal with these groups, and turn the fire of the whole of the rest of your platoon on to the main body. You must be careful to see that all your men lie down, that no one but yourself has his head above ground level, and you must camouflage yourself. The suspense in such a situation as this makes great demands on the men's discipline, and they are apt to look up and be seen by the enemy, thus destroying all hope of surprise.

PROBLEM 5*b*

The situation is exactly the same as in Problem 5*a*, except that instead of a platoon advancing towards you, there is a whole company marching in fours, with four groups 100 yards in front of it.

What action would you take?

Action considered Correct.

Exactly the same as in Problem 5*a*. The enemy is in this case four times as strong as you are, but the effect of surprise should more than make up for this, and the first minute after you open fire should decide the action in your favour.

PROBLEM 5*c*

The situation is again exactly the same as in 5*a* and 5*b*, except that a whole battalion with eight groups 200 yards in front of it is advancing.

What action would you take?

Action considered Correct.

In this case the situation is changed. You are an outpost, and your first duty is to warn your main body in case of an attack and to give it time to prepare itself. It is just possible that if you allow the battalion to approach to within 300 yards you might deal it such a blow as to almost destroy it; but if, on the contrary, the covering groups were composed of really good soldiers and the companies were well commanded, there would be a great chance of your being rushed, and this is a risk which you ought not to take, for it would compromise the whole situation. In these circumstances you should therefore take steps to open a rapid fire on the enemy immediately with your men and your Lewis gun. Your object in doing this would be to keep him at arm's length and delay his advance as much as possible so as to give your supports and reserves time to prepare themselves.

Your affectionate father,
"X. Y. Z."

LETTER VII

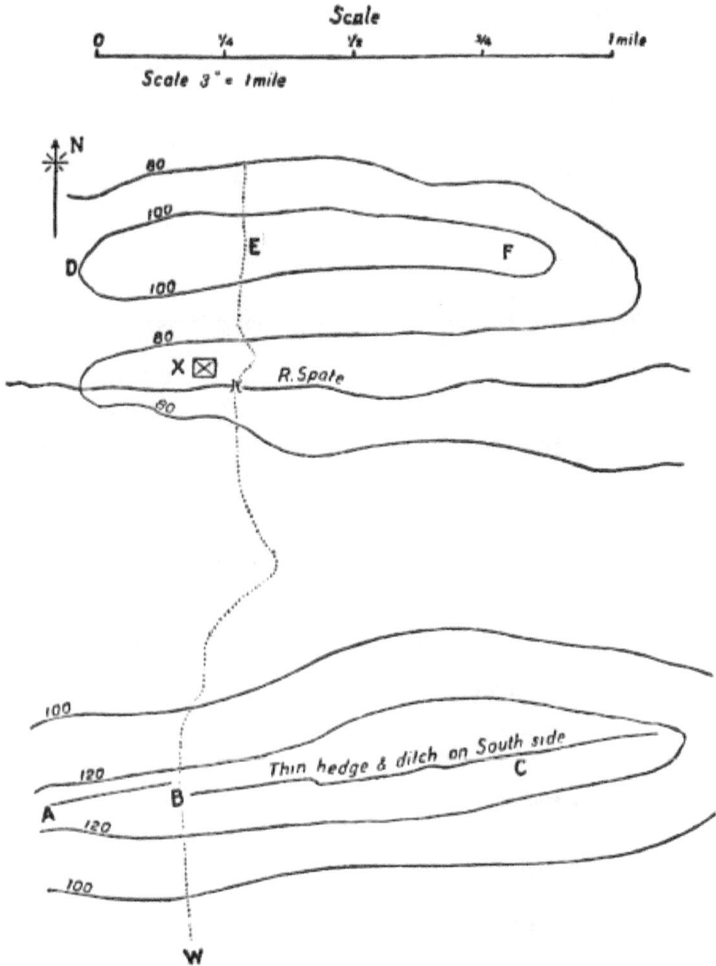

January 15, 1918.

Problem 6

My dear Dick,—

In this letter I am going to set you another fire problem. It is one in which, presuming that the men are fairly well trained in musketry, everything depends on the orders given by the company commander.

You are in command of a company and are marching in a northerly direction along the road *W B E*, with scouts in front of you. On reaching the top of the ridge at *B* your scouts halt and beckon to you. You go forward and see what appears to be an enemy's battalion at *X*, by the bank of the River Spate. The battalion is in close column and the men are lying down resting. The country all round the battalion is open. There is a thin hedge on the top of the ridge *A B C* through which you can see and through which you could fire, but which gives you cover from view.

State how the situation presents itself to you and also give your exact orders.

Solution considered Correct.

You should reason with yourself as follows:

"If I advance beyond the hedge I shall be seen and my company will be opposed by a battalion. There seems to be an excellent opportunity of surprising the enemy, who shows no sign of moving, with my concentrated fire, and I shall consequently make my plans deliberately. From my map I judge the distance from the top of the ridge to the bridge over the River Spate to be 1,300 yards, and the centre of the battalion about 1,400 yards, but as I want to be quite sure of getting the battalion into my bracket, I shall use combined sights. I shall first line up the whole company 30 yards behind the hedge, and then order No. 1 Platoon to fix their sights at 1,300, No. 2 at 1,400, No. 3 at 1,500, and No. 4 at 1,600 yards, with the Lewis gun of No. 1 Platoon at 1,350, that of No. 2 at 1,400, that of No. 3 at 1,450, and that of No. 4 at 1,500 yards. I shall then order the whole company to creep up into position, and when the target has been properly pointed out I shall blow my whistle, on which every man will fire twenty rounds rapid and each Lewis gun six drums. At the end of the twenty rounds I can, if necessary, correct my ranges. Men are, as a rule, more apt to fire high than low, and I should have given the ranges 1,200, 1,300, 1,400, 1,500, instead of 1,300, 1,400, 1,500, 1,600, had it not been that the river will prevent the enemy rushing straight towards me if he finds the fire is high, whereas if my ranges are short he could get out of range by retiring."

Your affectionate father,
"X. Y. Z."

LETTER VIII

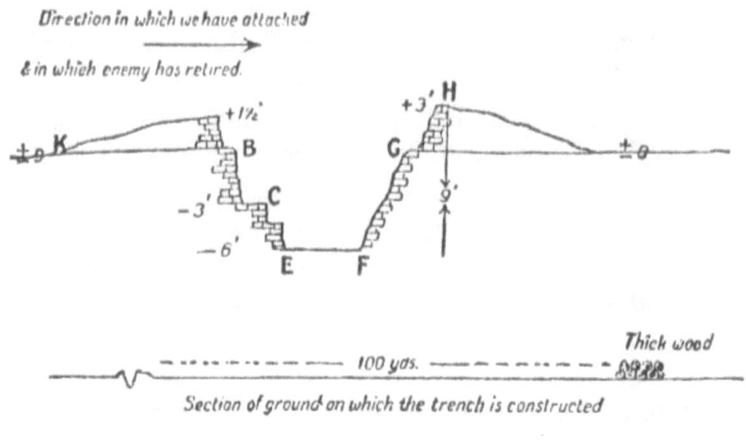

January 22, 1918.

PROBLEM 7

MY DEAR DICK,—

The following is a problem in trench warfare such as you may be called upon to solve any day in the trenches.

The company of which you are in command has succeeded in getting into a trench a section of which is given in the diagram. It has only incurred about 10 per cent. of casualties. The trench is the last of the German system, and there is a clear field of fire for about 100 yards in the direction in which the enemy has retired; after that there is a thick wood.

Your telephone communication has broken down and it is evident that you will for some time have to rely on your own resources. Your flanks are secured by troops on your right and left. Your company now numbers 120 rank and file. The front allotted to you measures about 150 yards. The trench which you are now occupying was considerably shelled by us previous to its capture, and what was the rear of the trench when the Germans held it, namely $H\,G\,F$, has been considerably broken down in half a dozen places. It is quite possible that the Germans will counter-attack from the wood without delay. It is evident from the section of the trench depicted on the diagram that you cannot fire out of it as it is at present.

Problem.

What action will you take to prepare for the enemy's counter-attack?

Solution considered Correct.

Your position is a difficult one, for there is no place from which your men can fire. You cannot even use the step C, nor the parapet $A\,K$, for the parados $H\,G$ is, as is usually the case, eighteen inches higher than is the old crest line at A. In the short time at your disposal it will be next to impossible to make a continuous step so as to enable you to fire over H, and in the circumstances the best thing for you to do is to concentrate the whole of your energies on getting your Lewis guns into position and to use intensive labour for the purpose.[1] It is possible that you may be able to get one or two of the Lewis guns satisfactorily into position at some of the places in which the revetment in $F\,G\,H$ has been knocked down. If, in your company, you have half a dozen iron or wire grips which you can utilise to pull down the sandbag revetment, you will find them of the greatest assistance, for men who only have their hands to work with find it very difficult to get a grip on a sandbag which is in a revetment.

You must at once place look-out men to give you warning of any sign of the enemy assembling in the edge of the wood to your front and be prepared to open on them with rifle grenades.

The real advantage that a machine gun or Lewis gun has over a rifle is that from a small point of vantage one of these weapons can pour a tremendous hail of fire, and in such circumstances as those depicted above there is no doubt but that the first consideration should be to get your Lewis guns into position.

If possible, it is best to place these in pairs, shooting obliquely and crossing their fire in front of you. As soon as this is done you should thin out and organise your defence in depth. This being carried out, you must determine what localities you will hold and where you will have your gaps. You should generally have a locality in front of any communication trench leading up from the rear. As soon as you have determined on your localities, you must set-to and build a fire step. The next measure to take in order of importance is to collect ammunition and place it at convenient points. After you have done this, try to put wire or some other obstacle in front. In advising this, I am presuming that you have reached your final objective. Be careful to remove any old German wire behind you which will prevent your own supports coming up over the open to reinforce you. Try to get your localities marked by lamps at night, that your own friends in rear can see where they are.

Problem 8

After hard fighting you have driven the enemy out of the trench *A B C*, and he has retired up the communication trench *D E F* in the direction of his supports. You are in command of a platoon and have been ordered to take steps to prevent the enemy again advancing along the communication trench *E D B*. It is not the intention of your commanding officer to advance at present any farther than the points he has already reached. The time is an hour before dark.

What steps will you take to carry out the instructions you have received?

Solution considered Correct.

Pull knife-rests[2] down into the trench *D E F*, also throw wire into it if available. At once put a couple of men at the point *D* to cover the trench *D E* with their rifles. As soon as you are able to do so, dig a short trench from *G* to *D* and place a Lewis gun at *G* to enfilade *D E*. You may have to wait until after dark before you actually carry this out, but you should make arrangements for doing it by daylight. It would not be a bad plan to tie a few tins on to the knife-rests which you have thrown into the trench, so that the rattle, if they are moved, will give you warning of any one's approach. The Lewis gun at *G* will be practically out of bombing range from *E F*.

[2] A knife-rest is a portable wire entanglement about 10 feet long, made upon a wooden frame-work.

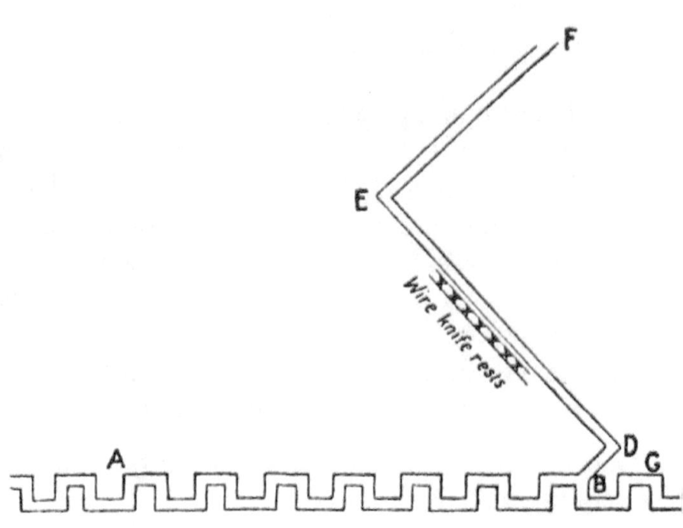

* * * * *

There are as many different types of stops as there are different sorts of trenches. Some of these types are better than others, but there is no type which is suitable under all circumstances. Everything must depend on the exact local conditions and on the means at your disposal. It does not require much ingenuity to devise a good stop for a trench if you have leisure to think the matter out, but just as a remark which would be commonplace if given as the result of matured deliberation is regarded as brilliant if made as a quick repartee, so in tactics to do what is right under fire is quite a different thing to answering a question on an examination paper. Nevertheless, to have answered a similar question on an examination paper, or, still better, to have done it as a tactical exercise, renders it very much more likely that you will do the right thing when you are faced by a similar problem in earnest. I, therefore, counsel you to carefully consider the different sorts of trenches which you come across and to think out carefully how you would put a stop in them, or how you turn them to shoot in the opposite direction. In the diagram I have given you it is just possible that by cutting down the elbow at *E*, you may be able to enfilade the section of trench *E F* from *A*. This would, however, depend on the ground and on the actual construction of the trenches concerned.

Your affectionate father,
"X. Y. Z."

LETTER IX

February 1, 1918.

PROBLEM 9

MY DEAR DICK,—

This week my letter will be a short one, as it only contains one very simple problem.

You are on outpost duty and have been told that the General is very anxious to get one or two live prisoners. Your picquet is at some cross-roads a quarter of a mile south of the road *A B* marked on the map. You have reason to believe that it is probable that the enemy will patrol down the road *A B*. *A B* is a good road with strong fences on either side of it, and with ditches on the road side of the fence.

Does any special way of taking prisoners alive in this road suggest itself to you?

Solution.

A very good plan to adopt in these circumstances would be what the Japanese used to call the trap-door. If your post consists of six men, leave four under the leader at *A* and tell them to conceal themselves in the ditch, and place two, also concealed in the ditch, forty yards in front of the mat *B*. If the enemy's patrol comes along, the men at *B* should allow it to pass them and then give a signal and at the same time themselves take steps to cut off the patrol's retreat, whilst the four men at *A* prevent it advancing farther.

* * * * *

The above little scheme is so simple that I should feel that I ought to apologise for setting it, were it not that I am quite certain that three out of four of your comrades to whom you may set it will not give the proper solution.

I saw a similar little problem given to men of different regiments in India. The only troops who answered it properly were Pathans. It apparently much resembles traps which they set for one another in their inter-tribal fights. Although some twenty teams competed, neither British troops, Sikhs, Hindustani, Mohammedans, nor Rajputs ever managed to successfully catch their men.

Your affectionate father,
"X. Y. Z."

LETTER X

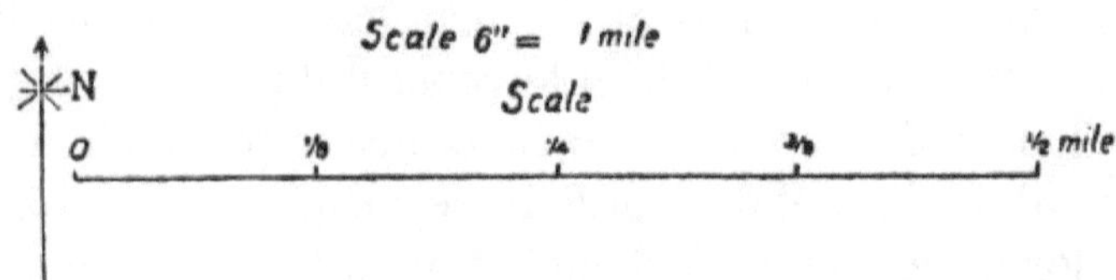

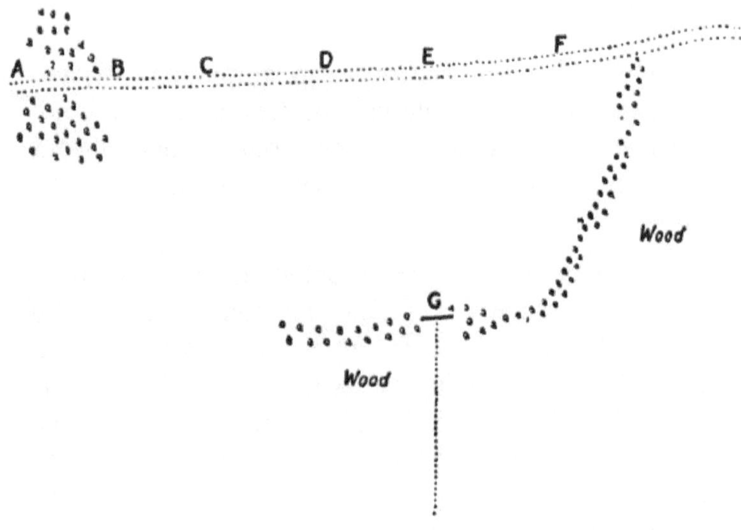

February 7, 1918.

PROBLEM 10

My dear Dick,—

The problem I am setting you to-day has to do with fire control.

You are on outpost facing in a northerly direction and are in command of a picquet consisting of the headquarters of a platoon with a Lewis gun and thirty men at *G*. A man who has been sent in from a group on your left tells you that a company of the enemy is moving across your front from left to right along the road *A B C D E F*. He says that the company is marching with an advanced guard of one platoon about 200 yards in front of it. The platoon has a couple of groups 200 yards in front of it again. Five minutes after you have received this notice, you see a group of the enemy marching from the wood at *B*.

Problem.

How do you appreciate the situation and what action do you intend to take?

Solution.

So long as you remain carefully concealed at *G* and your men do not show themselves, it is at least as likely as not that the enemy's scouts will not discover you. If, however, they should do so, your danger will come from the enemy's company and the platoon in front of it and not from the scouts, and it is with these larger bodies that you must make your plans to deal. At this close range you ought to be able to put them out of action in the first minute after opening fire. If your men conceal themselves properly, even if the scouts do discover you, they will not do so until the enemy's main body is nearing the point *C*. Your orders should consequently be somewhat as follows:

"Let every man conceal himself.

"The Lewis gun and Nos. 1 and 2 Sections of the platoon on my command to open fire will direct their fire half left on the main body of the enemy's company, which will be the rearmost party. No. 3 Section will deal with the platoon forming the advanced guard, and No. 4 Section, taking its orders from the section commander, will deal with isolated groups. No man will put up his head until I give the order to fire. The whole platoon will use fixed sights."

You should at once issue these preliminary orders. If you are not discovered, do not open fire until the head of the main body has reached *D*.

Napoleon used to say that if you ever saw your enemy making a mistake, you should give him lots of time to make it thoroughly before punishing him. Do not pull the bait out of the pike's mouth until he has properly gorged it. This maxim applies equally whether you are dealing with armies or only with platoons. I, myself, remember in my early days missing a tiger sixty yards off, when, if I had only waited, he would have walked right under the tree on which I was seated.

Your affectionate father,
"X. Y. Z."

LETTER XI

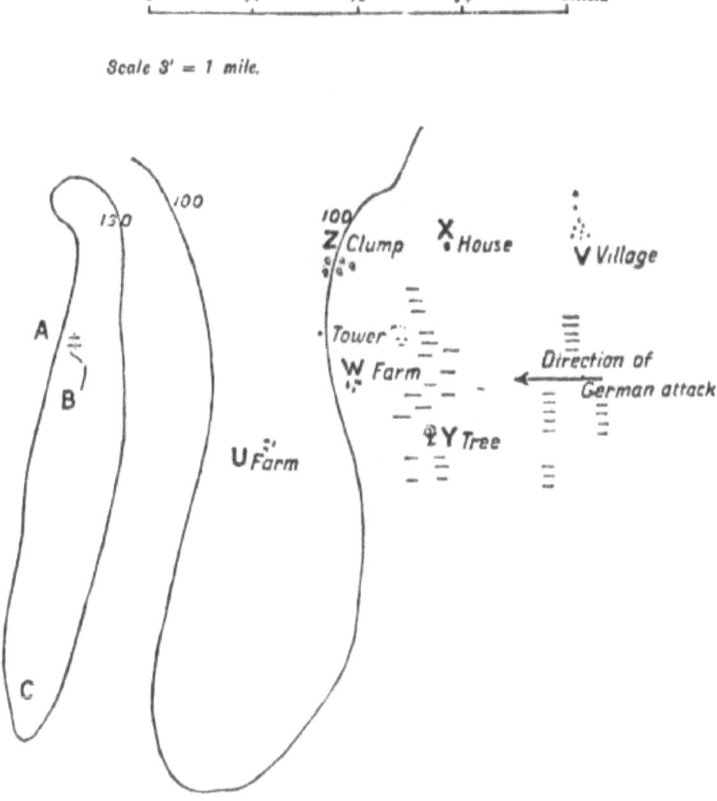

February 10, 1918.

MY DEAR DICK,—

I hope you will master and remember the principles which govern the problem I am setting you to-day. Although very simple, it requires a little more thought than most of those which have preceded it.

The Germans have broken through our front line. Your company, with its four Lewis guns and with four

Vickers guns which have been placed under your command, has been hastily thrown into the trench *B*, which is well constructed and well concealed, and has a good field of fire to the east. Four 18-pounder guns were in action at a hundred yards north of the trench *B*, but two of these guns have already been put out of action by the enemy's artillery. The Germans are advancing in great numbers regardless of sacrifice and are now about a mile distant. Their object is evidently to take the ridge *A C*, and it is of the utmost importance that they should be frustrated in their endeavours. The front allotted to you to defend runs from *Z* Clump on the north to *U* Farm on the south. Other troops are responsible outside these limits. You have in the trench *B* 50,000 rounds of ammunition besides that which the men have on them. You are senior to the officer in command of the remaining two 18-pounders.

What action would you take? and give your reasons.

Comments on the Situation and Action adjudged Correct.

Let us first of all consider how many rounds a minute you could expect the troops under your command to fire in the following circumstances:

(*a*) If the fire were only to be continued for two minutes.

(*b*) If it were to be kept up for half an hour.

Rounds.

(*a*) If it were to be kept up for two minutes only, you might expect 100 infantrymen to fire from fifteen to twenty rounds a minute (let us say)   3,200

Four Lewis guns to fire 600 rounds each in the two
minutes   2,400

Four Vickers to fire 750 rounds each in two minutes   3,000

8,600

(*b*) If the fire were to be kept up for half an hour you
might justly expect infantry to fire at an average
rate of five rounds a minute   15,000

It would be unwise to attempt to exceed this average
rate of fire, for even if your men were muscularly
able to continue firing at a greater rate, it is a known
thing that the nervous strain of firing is such that
there are but few men who can fire 200 rounds
consecutively without breaking down, and it is of
paramount importance that you should keep a
certain amount of reserve force in hand in case the
enemy gets to a really close range.

Four Lewis guns would during the half-hour be able to
fire 600 rounds each, and if these rounds were fired
at fairly long ranges would still be in a position to
fire 600 rounds rapid when the enemy got to close
quarters. The platoon commanders would,
however, be well advised to regard these Lewis
guns as their reserves and to do nothing to risk their
being ready to fire 600 rounds at the critical
moment. They should, therefore, use them very
sparingly at medium ranges   2,400

Four Vickers Maxims should be able to fire at an
average rate of 200 rounds a minute   24,000

In other words, in the two minutes you could fire at
the average rate of over 4,000 rounds a minute, but for
half an hour could only keep up an average rate of
about 800 rounds a minute. Another thing to be
considered is that your average of hits at the closer
ranges would be greater than they would be at the
farther ranges. There is, however, no reason why you

should not inflict as much loss as possible on the enemy at medium and long ranges, provided you know at what distance to fire. We used to consider in South Africa that when we were advancing against a position held by the enemy, he used to shoot straighter at 500 yards than he did at 200, for, fine shots as the Boers were, their excitement at our near approach disturbed their accurate shooting. You may therefore expect that your men will shoot *comparatively* better when the enemy is at medium ranges than when he is very close, provided that they know the distance.

It cannot be expected that you will go in for such a long disquisition at a moment when you are called upon to act, but you should have considered these points beforehand, at all events to such an extent that you would have decided to open fire when the enemy was still at comparatively long ranges, but to increase this fire as he got closer and to reserve the maximum rate of fire until you can pour it in with deadly effect. You must always remember that you are dealing with human beings who have nerves and not with machines. As I have previously said, the above principles should be those on which you decide to act, but the first thing you should do would be to send to the officer commanding the section of guns and inquire from him the ranges of any objects within rifle shot which he has ascertained, and you should at the same time desire him to obtain for you the ranges of any other prominent objects near which the enemy must pass, so that if his remaining guns are knocked out you will know what sights to use. Whilst this is being done, you should divide your front between your platoon commanders. The Lewis guns should remain with their platoons, but you would be wise to keep the Vickers Maxims under your own special command, so that you can turn them on to any portion of the advancing line which seems especially to threaten you. In fact, you should look on these as your reserve. Having thus considered the situation, you should issue the following orders:

"Fire fronts are allotted as under:

No. 1 Platoon to the right of Farm *U*.

No. 2 Platoon from farm *U* to *Y* tree.

No. 3 Platoon from *Y* tree to farm *W*.

No. 4 Platoon to the left of farm *W*."

Order No. 2.—"Ranges are being ascertained from the artillery and will be passed to platoon commanders. Platoon commanders can open fire at their own discretion, but must bear in mind the enormous importance of being ready in all respects to use the full power of their fire should the enemy succeed in getting to close ranges. The four Vickers Maxim guns will, under my orders, fire at any portion of the enemy's advance which appears to be especially threatening."

The majority of regimental officers now serving do not at all appreciate the enormous effect of rifle and machine-gun fire at medium and long ranges, nor the importance of taking every step in their power to obtain the accurate ranges as soon as they have taken up a position. The effect of the fire of a fairly good company in such circumstances as those above depicted and acting on the above carefully considered fire orders would be enormous, whereas if the fire fronts were not properly allotted and if ranges were unknown, it would be of comparatively little value.

Your affectionate father,
"X. Y. Z."

LETTER XII

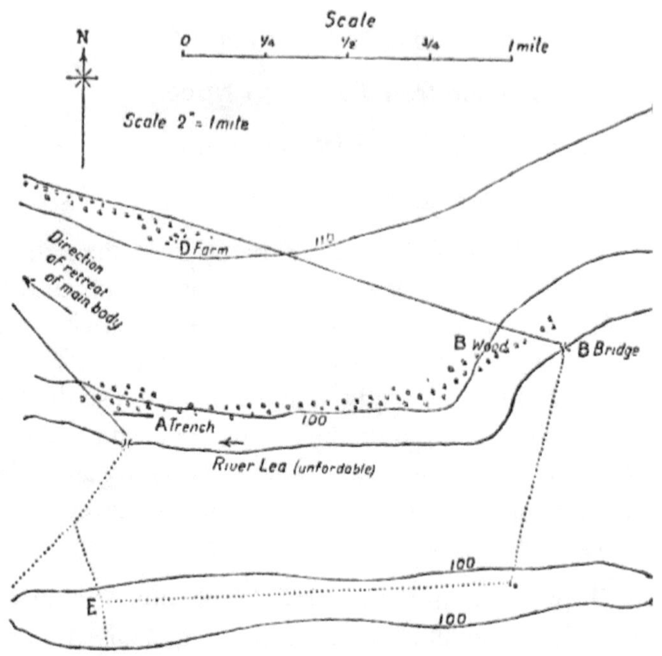

February 20, 1918.

MY DEAR DICK,—

What would you do in the following circumstances?

A force is retiring in a north-westerly direction. The River Lea shown on the map is unfordable. Two companies are acting as the point of the rearguard. Their orders are to hold the bridges at *A* and *B*. The bridge at *B* is to be held until 10 a.m. and the bridge at *A* until 10.30 a.m. If they can hold out until these hours, it is estimated that it will enable the main body to get away unmolested. The trees shown on the map are mostly oak, and are on an average forty feet high. The roads marked on the map are metalled and good. The farm buildings at *D* are strong. You are commanding B Company of your battalion, which is at *B* bridge, and are senior to Captain A., a reliable officer, who is occupying *A* trench just south of *A* wood. At 9.15 a.m. two scouts mounted on motor bicycles inform you that they have patrolled to the front and that none of the enemy are within three miles of you except a few companies near *E*, who are acting as support to an attack which is being made against *A* bridge. At 9.20 a.m. you receive the following message from Captain A., dated 9 a.m.: "Please do whatever you can to support me. I am being heavily shelled, and infantry are trying to push across *A* bridge. I fear that there is no chance of my being able to hold out until 10.30 a.m."

What action would you take? State your reasons for the manner in which you would act and then definitely say what you intend to do.

Comments on the Situation and Action adjudged Correct.

What you should always aim at is to obey the spirit of an order rather than its letter. You know Captain A. to be a reliable officer, and he says that he fears that he cannot hold out until 10.30. If the enemy seize *A* trench before that hour, not only will your retreat be cut off, but the object of ordering A and B Companies to hold the bridges so as to enable the main body to get a good start will be defeated. The nearest hostile infantry to you, at *E*, is some two miles off, that is to say, some forty minutes' march. In the circumstances it is your duty to go to the assistance of A Company. The next thing is to consider how you can best help him to carry out his retirement and also how you can best prevent the enemy from following up your main body. If you were to march straight to *A* wood, it is doubtful whether you would help him very materially. The artillery firing from the south of the river would deal with the reinforcements you brought up and placed in *A* trench, similarly to the way it dealt with B Company. By far your better plan will be to march as quickly as possible to *D* wood and occupy the strong buildings at *D* farm. From the farm buildings you will be able to prevent the enemy marching along the road from *A* to *X*, and should be able to comply with the spirit of the order, and by the delay you will thus entail on the enemy's movements you will be able to effect the same purpose as if you had actually prevented him from crossing *A* bridge before 10.30. You should be able to hold on to *D* farm until artillery are brought up to *A* wood, and should then be able to slip away along the road *B X*. Without aeroplane observation, hostile artillery could not observe the effect of their fire from the S. of the river, as trees intercept their view.

Orders.

B Company will at once march to *D* wood and occupy *D* farm.

Order to Officer Commanding A Company.

I am marching immediately to *D* farm, which I hope to reach before 10 a.m. From this place I shall be in a position to facilitate your retreat and prevent your being pursued farther than *A* wood. You may retire as soon as you see that I have established myself in the farm buildings. Having accomplished the object for which we have been sent out, I shall continue my retirement to *X*.

* * * * *

These twelve little schemes I have set you are, as I think you will admit, all very simple, but I am willing to wager that you have not answered all of them correctly, even though they were only applications of the axioms which I gave in the letter which preceded them. The difficulty is, in the heat of the moment, to decide correctly which of the axioms deals with the special situation, and nothing but practice will get over this difficulty.

You should always take every opportunity of discussing with your comrades little tactical situations which have occurred, or those which may occur. In talking over the former, do not do so with the object of passing censure, but merely with the view of learning what to do and what not to do should you find yourself in a similar situation.

Whenever you have an opportunity, carefully explain the situation to your men. This is necessary if you expect them to co-operate intelligently in bringing about your designs.

In the solution of any little scheme which you may set to your subordinates, insist on definite orders being given and do not be content with vague disquisitions. When any little problem which you have set has been unsatisfactorily solved, let another leader fall in, take command, and do it again properly. This is the best way to ensure the proper solution being thoroughly understood and remembered for application on a future occasion. So long as you do not censure a superior in front of his men, it is a good thing to make your remarks in such a way that everybody can hear them.

You must guard against technical instructors giving wrong impressions. The bombing sergeant is inclined to impress on the men that there is no such weapon as the bomb. The instructors in the rifle grenade and the Lewis gun are also apt to talk so much of the value of the weapons in which they instruct that their pupils come away with very false ideas. The Lewis-gun sergeant, although he never fails to tell the men [95] that the Lewis gun can fire at the rate of 600 rounds a minute, very often does forget to inform them that after firing 600 rounds it takes twenty minutes or half an hour to cool before it is capable of firing any more. It is all very well for these men to be enthusiasts, but you must see that they abide strictly by the truth and avoid giving false impressions.

I will close this letter with a few remarks on the moral forces. As Napoleon said, these are, compared with the physical, as three is to one. Men's courage and determination and the will to conquer are more than half the battle. The situation to-day is no less serious than it was when I ended the last of my Twelve Letters to you, and it behoves you to devote the whole of your time and your energy to making yourself in every way efficient, and you must always bear in mind that it is possible that the little action in the winning or losing of which your right or wrong decision may be the principal factor may be the turning-point of a great battle.

Your affectionate father,
"X. Y. Z."